Rock It!™

Volcanoes and Earthquakes
Making and Moving Rock

Steven M. Hoffman

PowerKiDS press.
New York

Published in 2011 by The Rosen Publishing Group, Inc.
29 East 21st Street, New York, NY 10010

First Edition

Editor: Amelie von Zumbusch
Book Design: Kate Laczynski
Layout Design: Ashley Burrell

Photo Credits: Cover © www.iStockphoto.com/Warren Goldswain; p. 4 Ctein/Getty Images; p. 6 Hemera/Thinkstock; p. 8 Art Wolfe/Getty Images; p. 10 (main) © www.iStockphoto.com/Brytta; p. 10 (inset) © www.iStockphoto.com/Christopher Nuzzaco; p. 12 I Love Photo and Apple/Getty Images; p. 14 Joe Raedle/Staff/Getty Images; p. 16 Stocktrek/Getty Images; p. 18 Tom Pfeiffer/Volcano Discovery/Getty Images; p. 20 © www.iStockphoto.com/Youding Xie.

Library of Congress Cataloging-in-Publication Data

Hoffman, Steven M. (Steven Michael), 1960–
Volcanoes and earthquakes : making and moving rock / by Steven M. Hoffman. — 1st ed.
p. cm. — (Rock it!)
Includes index.
ISBN 978-1-4488-2559-2 (library binding) — ISBN 978-1-4488-2704-6 (pbk.) —
ISBN 978-1-4488-2705-3 (6-pack)
1. Volcanoes—Juvenile literature. 2. Volcanism—Juvenile literature. 3. Earthquakes—Juvenile literature. I. Title.
QE521.3.H64 2011
551.21—dc22

2010030258

Manufactured in the United States of America

CPSIA Compliance Information: Batch #WW11PK: For Further Information contact Rosen Publishing, New York, New York at 1-800-237-9932

CONTENTS

This lava flow is from Kilauea, a volcano on the island of Hawaii. Kilauea is one of Earth's most active volcanoes.

Active Earth

Like a big red fountain, hot **lava** bursts from a mountain and falls to the ground. The volcano has awakened! Some of the lava cools quickly. This cooling lava forms pieces of rock. The **eruption** continues. A river of lava flows down the mountain's side. In time, this lava will harden into rock, as well.

Erupting volcanoes show that Earth is an active planet. Though it has a cool, rocky outside, Earth is very hot inside. Heat from inside Earth causes many changes. The eruption of a volcano is one of these changes. An earthquake is another. In earthquakes, pieces of Earth's outside push past each other. The ground shakes far and wide.

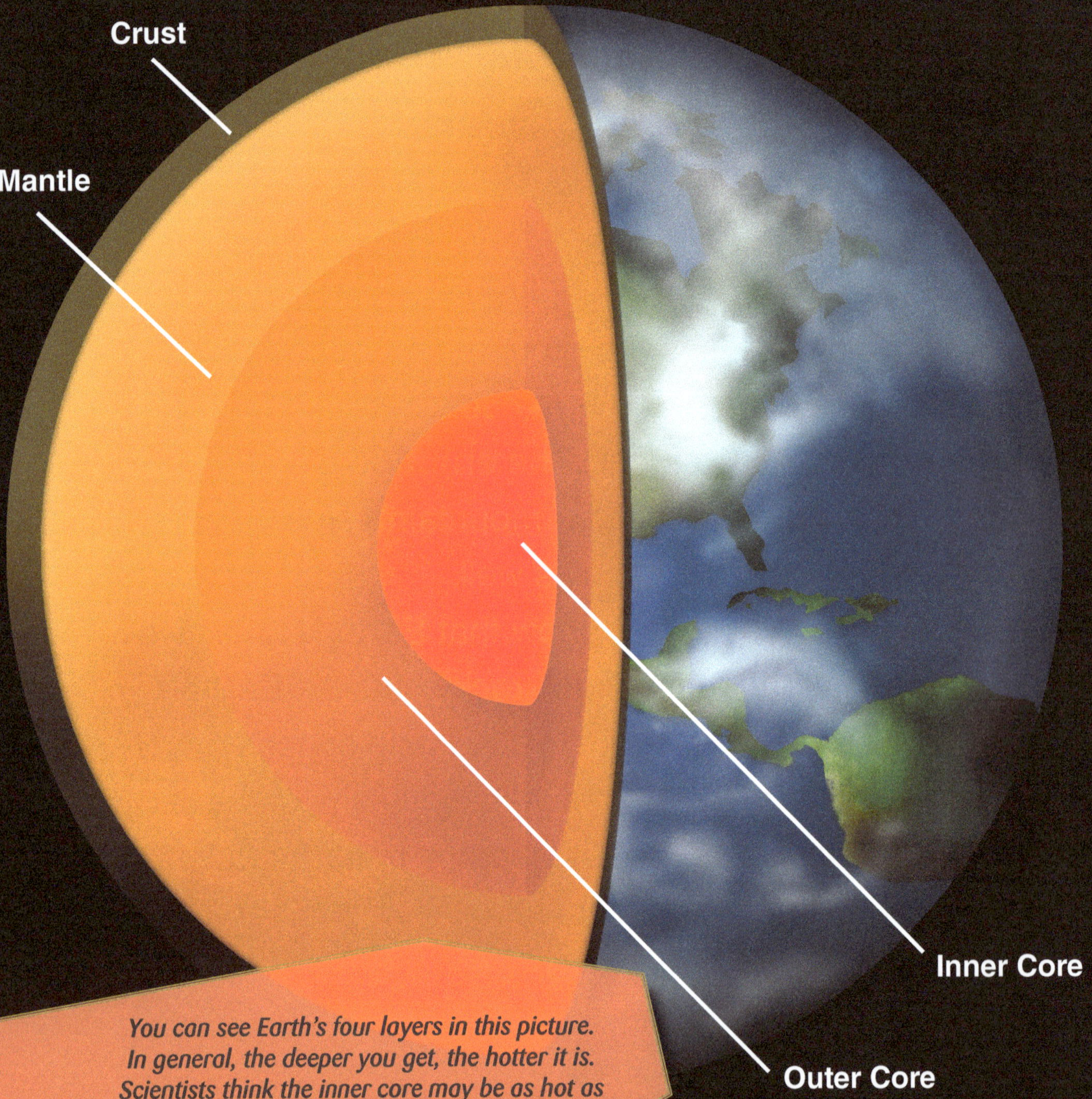

You can see Earth's four layers in this picture. In general, the deeper you get, the hotter it is. Scientists think the inner core may be as hot as 9,000° F (4,982° C)!

Layers of Earth

Earth has several layers. The **core** is the deepest and hottest layer. Its inside is solid metal because of the huge weight of the matter above it. The core's outside is made of melted metal.

The next layer up is the **mantle**. It is made of rock that melts into **magma** at some places.

The **crust** is Earth's outer layer. Its rock is cool and breaks fairly easily. The crust is broken into pieces, called plates. There are about 20 plates, some large and some small. The plates slide slowly over a hot, slippery part of Earth's mantle. Their movement can make magma form. It also causes earthquakes.

This lava is from an eruption of Kilauea. The lava is a kind of lava called pahoehoe. Pahoehoe has smooth, ropy bumps.

Lava from Below

Volcanoes form above places where rock in Earth's mantle or crust has melted into magma. The magma may pool under the volcano. The volcano erupts when the magma pushes hard enough to break through the rock above it.

Volcanoes erupt in different ways. Sticky magma has lots of gas mixed into it. It erupts like the soda in a shaken can. Lava breaks apart and is thrown high into the air. Small bits of lava cool and fall as **ash**. Thinner magma lets most of the gas escape. It erupts gently as a fountain or a smooth lava flow.

Melted rock is known as magma when it is underground. Once it breaks through Earth's crust, it is called lava.

Basalt sometimes forms tall columns, like these. Inset: The igneous rock pumice forms from lava that was full of air. Pumice has holes and is light enough to float in water.

Lava to Rock

When they cool, lava and magma form **igneous rocks**. There are several kinds of igneous rocks. Some are glassy. Others have small or large **crystals**.

Lava that erupts onto Earth's surface cools quickly. It may cool so quickly that volcanic glass forms. The shiny, black rock obsidian forms this way. If lava cools more slowly, rocks with small **mineral** crystals form. Two rocks that form this way are basalt and rhyolite.

Magma cools very slowly beneath Earth's surface. Rocks that form underground from magma have large crystals. The rocks gabbro and granite form this way.

Volcanic ash that falls to Earth often becomes a rock called tuff.

This volcano is Fuji, in Japan. It is a composite volcano. Composite volcanoes are also sometimes known as stratovolcanoes.

Making Mountains

The rock that forms in volcanic eruptions builds volcanic mountains. Shield volcanoes are large, shield-shaped volcanic mountains. They grow slowly from flows of runny lava that harden into rock one layer on top of another.

Composite volcanoes form from flows of sticky lava and eruptions of ash. The sticky lava does not flow well. It piles into a tall, steep mountain. Ash layers occur between the many lava flows.

Cinder cone volcanoes are smaller. They are made of unevenly shaped pieces of black or red rock, called cinders. Cinders form when pieces of lava cool in the air. The cinders pile up into a cone shape.

During an earthquake, buildings and bridges may break apart and fall down. On March 10, 2010, an earthquake destroyed this bridge in Chile.

Shake, Rattle, and Roll

Earthquakes move rocks, including those formed by volcanoes. Most earthquakes occur when large blocks of rock slide along cracks in Earth's crust. These cracks are called **faults**.

Many faults have uneven edges. These keep the blocks of rock on each side of a fault from slipping smoothly past each other. Instead, the blocks bend. Energy is stored in the bent rock, just as it is in a bent ruler. When the force of the rocks pushing against each other becomes too large, the fault breaks. The rock on each side moves and snaps back to its unbent shape. The energy is released as an earthquake.

This is California's San Andreas Fault. There have been several earthquakes along the fault, including ones in 1857, 1906, and 1989.

Faults of Earth

Scientists divide faults into three basic types. The type depends on how the two blocks of rock move compared to each other. In a normal fault, a block of rock slides down a lower block of rock. A reverse fault is the opposite of a normal fault. One block of rock is pushed up over a lower block of rock.

A strike-slip fault is a fault along which rocks slip sideways past each other. One famous strike-slip fault is California's San Andreas Fault. In 1906, an earthquake along this fault destroyed much of San Francisco.

Some faults include many smaller, related faults that together allow movement. These are called fault zones.

Merapi, seen here, is one of the most active volcanoes on the island of Java, in Indonesia. Merapi is part of the Ring of Fire, around the Pacific Ocean.

Ring of Fire

Some faults are weak points within Earth's plates. Other faults are plate boundaries, or places where two plates meet. When the plates slide past each other, earthquakes occur. Where plates push together, one plate may sink beneath another. The scraping of the sinking plate causes earthquakes.

A sinking plate also makes rock melt. The melted rock may erupt in a volcano. Volcanoes also form at places where plates pull apart. Lava fills the gap between the plates.

Many plate boundaries are along the shores of the Pacific Ocean. Many volcanoes and earthquakes occur there. The volcanoes form a ring known as the Ring of Fire.

This building in China's Sichuan Province was destroyed by a big earthquake on May 12, 2008. Sadly, many people died in the earthquake.

Danger from Below

Volcanic eruptions present many dangers. The lava from an erupting volcano can flow over houses or roads. Eruptions also make snow and ice at the tops of volcanic mountains melt. This causes large **mudflows**. Explosive volcanic eruptions release hot ash and gases that flow down the mountain quickly. These can make it hard for people to breathe.

Earthquakes are a danger, too. The shaking of a strong earthquake can make buildings and bridges fall down. Fires sometimes start when earthquakes break gas lines or knock over wood-burning stoves. Earthquakes on the ocean floor can cause huge waves, called **tsunamis**.

Warnings of Danger

Scientists watch many volcanoes. They record **data** on the most active volcanoes at all times. They use the data to warn people when a volcano is likely to erupt. The warnings can come days or even months before an eruption.

Scientists study earthquakes, too. They use machines to record the shaking caused by earthquakes. The machines can also sense small shakings that occur right before big earthquakes. This lets the scientists set off sirens several seconds before the strong shaking begins.

Volcanic eruptions and earthquakes can be scary. During one, always listen to warnings and follow directions. Doing so will keep you safe.

GLOSSARY

ash (ASH) Pieces of tiny rock that shoot out of a volcano when it erupts.

core (KOR) The hot center of Earth.

crust (KRUST) The outer, or top, layer of a planet.

crystals (KRIS-tulz) Hard, clear matter that has points and flat sides.

data (DAY-tuh) Facts.

eruption (ih-RUP-shun) The explosion of gases, smoke, or lava from a volcano.

faults (FAWLTS) Breaks in Earth's rocky outside.

igneous rocks (IG-nee-us ROKS) Hot, liquid, underground minerals that have cooled and hardened.

lava (LAH-vuh) Hot, melted rock that comes out of a volcano.

magma (MAG-muh) Hot, melted rock inside Earth.

mantle (MAN-tul) The middle layer of Earth.

mineral (MIN-rul) Natural matter that is not an animal, a plant, or another living thing.

mudflows (MUD-flohz) Heavy flows of mud and dirt.

tsunamis (soo-NAH-meez) Groups of waves caused by movements in Earth's crust on the ocean floor.

INDEX

WEB SITES

Due to the changing nature of Internet links, PowerKids Press has developed an online list of Web sites related to the subject of this book. This site is updated regularly. Please use this link to access the list:
www.powerkidslinks.com/rockit/volcano/